Comprehension Activities
for Reading in Social Studies and Science

By LeAnn Nickelsen

SCHOLASTIC
PROFESSIONAL BOOKS

New York • Toronto • London • Auckland • Sydney
Mexico City • New Delhi • Hong Kong • Buenos Aires

Thank you to:

Joel, my husband, for watching our children on the weekends.

My parents, Jim and Dolores Heim, for their constant support.

Keaton and Aubrey, my 19-month-old twins, for taking great naps so I could work.

Tina Dittrich, friend and teacher, for her great ideas and support.

Jeanette Moss, my editor, for doing such a great job of wording my ideas.

Virginia Dooley, my senior editor, for giving me this opportunity.

Edited by Jeanette Moss
Cover design by Jimmy Safarti
Interior design by Sydney Wright
ISBN 0-439-09838-6

Contents

Introduction

Integrating Reading Lessons into the Content Areas

Every year, teachers face the perennial problem: additions and changes to the curriculum that require more and more of their time, but no more time to teach. Yet there is a way to fit it all in: Integrate reading-skill instruction into the curriculum! Rather than rushing through social studies and science and then spending the rest of the time on *the basics*—reading, writing, and arithmetic—teachers can use expository (informational) school-mandated science and social studies books, along with trade books and other resources to integrate reading skills and strategies within the content areas.

Integration of content area curriculum with reading-skill development is a powerful technique. Not only is subject matter more interesting and accessible, but students are learning a lot more in less time because they are making new and interesting connections. You'll use the traditional textbooks that are subject and grade-level specific, along with a variety of resources. For example, the Civil War is part of many fifth-grade curriculums. Instead of just reading from the social studies book, find good historical fiction relating to the war. The war becomes more real because students see it through a character's point of view (usually one of their age). Then, have the students read a play and perform it. Now students' emotions are helping them to embed the information into their long-term memories.

This book will provide activities with supportive reproducibles to use before, during, and after reading.

> *"The most logical place for instruction in most reading and thinking strategies is in social studies and science rather than in separate lessons about reading. The reason is that the strategies are useful mainly when the student is grappling with important but unfamiliar content."*
>
> Becoming a Nation of Readers (1985)

Why Use Expository Text?

Expository, or informational, writings tend to be the most difficult for children to comprehend because they often deal with abstract, unfamiliar concepts. However, it's essential for students to learn content area reading strategies in order to comprehend factual material they will come across every day of their lives. Teaching students strategies to tackle expository writing will allow them to become content-literate students who can effectively read, focus attention on, comprehend, retain, and react to appropriate instructional materials in a given subject area at a given grade or ability level.

Remember how many of us were taught social studies and science in grade school—taking turns reading a paragraph and answering the four or five questions at the end of the chapter? I do. While my classmates were reading aloud, I remember focusing on what section I would probably read and thinking about how well I would read it. Unfortunately, I wasn't comprehending much.

By using the strategies in this book, you can help students succeed at reading expository material. They'll be able to break through the barriers to reading informational writing with skill and understanding. They will spend more time on social studies and science topics. They'll comprehend more and enjoy learning.

The Importance of Expository Texts

In her book *Classrooms That Work*, Patricia Cunningham says informational books are important because they

* answer questions.
* ask questions.
* encourage critical thinking.
* stimulate interest and curiosity.
* create a sense of wonder.
* develop understanding of people, places, and things.
* provide additional models and inspiration for writing.
* provide rich vocabulary.
* stimulate the making of connections.
* enlarge storage of background information.
* contain a variety of visuals (photos, drawings, maps, graphs, diagrams).
* reduce the fragmentation of the curriculum/day by creating links to math, science, and social studies.
* engage students in multiple ways of knowing/thinking/behaving (historical, scientific, mathematical).

Breaking Through Barriers to Comprehension

The following seven conditions can make reading expository text difficult:

- The reader has limited prior knowledge and experiences.

- The reader selects the wrong schema (how knowledge is stored and organized within the brain).

- The author provides inadequate text information.

- The reader has limited cultural experiences.

- The reader is unfamiliar with the text structure.

- The reader has limited vocabulary knowledge.

- The reader has a limited range of reading strategies.

> Comprehension is:
> * an active, constructive process;
> * a thinking process before, during, and after reading;
> * an interaction of the reader, the text, and the context.
>
> **Palinscar, Ogle, Jones, Carr & Ransom**
> **—Pamphlet**

Questions Provide Answers—and Focus

Questioning is a great way to have students focus on what is most important in the reading selection. Tailor the general questions below to the selection your students are reading. The questions will help your students think about their thinking (metacognition) and practice the reading strategies emphasized in this book.

Questions to Ask Before, During, and After Reading

Prereading Questions

* Preview the passage. What do you think it will be about?

* What are some things you already know about the topic?

* What are your reading goals? What do you hope to learn from this passage?

* What is your purpose for reading? What are you required to do with the information you learn from reading? How will this affect how well you read this passage?

* What strategies could you use as you read the passage to help you understand what you are reading?

* How will you know that you understood the message intended by the author?

During Reading Questions

* What do you think the main ideas of the passage are so far?

* What kind of graphic organizer would you use to begin organizing these ideas?

* What did you picture in your mind about these ideas while you were reading?

* Is the information in this passage similar to anything you have learned before? How?

* What are you wondering about at this point in your reading? Write down a question.

* What is your attitude toward reading the passage at this point? Do you need to modify any of your behaviors, attitudes, or resources in order to reach your goal?

Post-reading Questions

* What were the main ideas in this passage? Were your predictions accurate?

* What other information do you want to remember from this passage? How will you help yourself remember this information?

* Did you accomplish your reading goal?

* Which reading and teaming strategies did you find most helpful, and why?

* What parts of the passage interested you the most? What ideas made you think?

* How has your thinking changed as a result of reading this passage?

Getting Ready to Read Classroom Textbooks

The strategies and activities in Chapters 1, 2, and 3 of this book can be used with informational trade books and historical novels, as well as classroom social studies and science books. However, before we move to those activities, let's concentrate on the special aspects of reading content area textbooks. It's important to prepare students to get the most out of these classroom staples. Here's how:

- **Preview the text before reading it.** Look at titles, subheadings, bold and italicized type, maps, visuals, and so on. (See box on page 8.)

- **Sample the text prior to reading it.** This may include reading the first and last paragraphs of the section (introduction and conclusion).

- **Discuss what students might find within the section.** What are their questions, concerns, or thoughts so far? What do they already know about the topic of this section?

Textbook Preview

Your students will encounter various types of textbooks throughout their schooling. If you take the time to teach the following functions and characteristics, they'll have a good foundation for understanding how textbooks work. With your students, go over

* the functions of boldface type,
* the functions of italicized type,
* the functions of subheadings,
* the functions of a chapter introduction or preview section,
* how to find definitions of key terms,
* types of visual aids,
* how to find the main idea of a paragraph,
* what certain transition words mean (*moreover*, *however*, and so on),
* what certain punctuation marks mean (colon, semi-colon, and so on),
* the functions of questions in the margins,
* why they should look at chapter study questions BEFORE beginning to read the chapter.

Another way to help students understand what they read in textbooks is to help them pay attention to how these books are organized. Graphic organizers can enable your students to figure the meaning out for themselves, and what they learn themselves, they'll remember. See Chapter 4 (pages 53–64) for the six most common organizational patterns, as well as reproducibles for each.

Planning and Moving On

Once students understand the characteristics of textbooks and how informational books are organized, they're ready to move on to strategies and activities that are more fun and encourage them to be more creative and interact with the text. The rest of this book is devoted to activities that introduce such strategies to use before reading, during reading, and after reading. You can use these with any informational text material.

To plan effective content area reading lessons, I use the check-off sheet and either worksheet (see reproducibles on pages 9 and 10) to make sure I've covered all the bases.

Lesson Plan for Content Area Reading

Objectives:

Materials:

Anticipatory Set:

Purpose for Reading:

Assessment:

Background Information:

Key Vocabulary:

Reading Book:

Chapter: _____ **Pages:** _____

Title: _____

Activity/Graphic Organizer/Procedure:

Questions Before:

Questions During:

Questions After:

Teacher Check-Off Sheet

Before beginning the content area lesson, I have . . .

_____ written the objectives for the lesson and let the students know them too.

_____ previewed the text and determined key concepts and vocabulary that students need to know.

_____ included activities and strategies that will help students develop a clear understanding of these key concepts.

_____ selected activities to assess, activate, and build students' background knowledge.

_____ identified the text's organizational pattern and found a graphic organizer to help students organize the material.

_____ decided the purpose that students should keep in mind while reading and prepared **before reading** questions that will help students read the text.

_____ told the students how they will be responsible for the information (quiz, test, writing assignment, project, discussion, and so on).

_____ developed **during reading** questions that will prompt students to create meaning with the information.

_____ created **after reading** questions and activities that require students to make meaningful connections and to deepen their understanding by applying what they have learned.

Comprehension Activities for Reading in Social Studies and Science Scholastic Professional Books

Chapter One

Before (and After) Reading Strategies

Why is it important to do anything about the reading before the reading begins? Because all learning is a response to what you already know and have experienced. People respond to new information by searching the mind for knowledge and understanding of what they already know in order to see how they can make the old meaning connect to the new. Words are processed according to what readers believe and know. Therefore, each reader will get something different out of the reading. If a student doesn't have any prior experiences or knowledge connected to the reading material, the text will be harder to understand and the vocabulary will be foreign.

Before reading a text, good readers will

* **activate prior knowledge** of the subject through reflection and prereading.

* **establish a realistic reading plan** after examining the assignment's length and difficulty through prereading.

* **understand the reading task** and set a clear purpose for reading.

* **create a productive study environment** and mind-set to accomplish their task.

Prereading activities motivate and prepare students to read. There are many strategies to choose from, so when you're deciding which will work best, think about the purpose for reading, the difficulty of the selection, and the background knowledge students may have. In their book *Scaffolding Reading Experiences*, Michael Graves and Bonnie Graves identified objectives for prereading activities: to motivate, to build or evoke background knowledge, to preteach vocabulary and concepts, to encourage prequestioning and prediction, to focus attention on text-specific knowledge, and to suggest effective strategies.

The following activities/strategies can be used within any subject. Each example gives an idea of how to use that strategy. Because most prereading activities are based on predicting and thinking ahead, many of them have an after-reading component. Students are eager to see how accurate their predictions were and to learn the answers to questions they had about the subject. The activities get them excited about learning, and the follow-up of checking their initial thinking piques their interest, reinforcing the information and building long-term memory. Although all of the strategies are reading strategies, I've grouped them into two subcategories: reading and vocabulary depending upon their particular focus.

READING STRATEGIES

Predict-o-Fact

Objective: To motivate students and elicit their background knowledge

Grouping: Independent

What to Do: Read the material ahead of time to identify the key points. Then work with students to list some predictions, "incorporating both true and false statements. Select four of these and write them on a copy of the "Predict-o-Fact" worksheet (page 18). Make a copy for each student and distribute. Ask students to use what they know or to make their best guesses and put a check mark under *True* or *False,* to the left of each prediction. Then, after they read the selection, have them place check marks under *True* or *False* to the right of each prediction. Encourage them to write a correct version of each false prediction and ask students to explain the evidence that made them change or keep their answers.

Name _____

Predict-o-Fact

Topic/Title _____

Take a picture and subheading walk through the book or chapter you are about to read, looking for clues to what it is about.

1. On each line below write a prediction sentence.

2. For each prediction put a check mark on the "Before Reading" true or false line according to what you think.

3. Read the selection.

4. Now put a check mark on the "After Reading" true or false line according to what you learned about each prediction.

5. Finally, write a corrected version of each false prediction on the line at the right.

Before Reading		Prediction	After Reading		Corrected Predictions
True	False		True	False	
—	—	_____	—	—	_____
—	—	_____	—	—	_____
—	—	_____	—	—	_____
—	—	_____	—	—	_____
—	—	_____	—	—	_____
—	—	_____	—	—	_____

Comprehension Activities for Reading in Social Studies and Science   Scholastic Professional Books, page 18

Concept Web

— Matrix

Objective: To motivate students and elicit their background knowledge

Grouping: Whole class

What to Do: Before each social studies or science unit, create a web that explains how all of the concepts introduced in the unit are tied together. Explain the web to students and tell them what they can look forward to doing with each concept (plays, simulations, projects, art, and so on). Then, in a class discussion, encourage them to add something to the web. This provides children with an opportunity to share what they know about the concept. You can do this before or after reading. Many additions are made after reading.

What's New?

Objective: To motivate students and elicit their background knowledge

Grouping: Independent, partners, or whole class

What to Do: Provide each child with a What's New? sheet on page 19. During a class discussion, have students share what they know about the future reading passage. Then talk about what you want them to know after they've read and have them write the objectives you've decided on in the space provided. After students read, have them write statements about what they did learn—including those objectives they were looking for as they read.

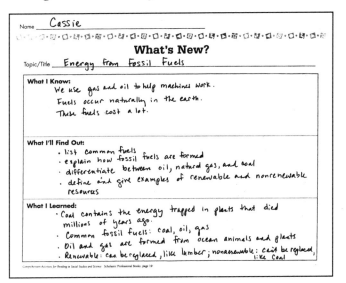

Name Cassie

What's New?

Topic/Title Energy from Fossil Fuels

What I Know:
We use gas and oil to help machines work.
Fuels occur naturally in the earth.
These fuels cost a lot.

What I'll Find Out:
· list common fuels
· explain how fossil fuels are formed
· differentiate between oil, natural gas, and coal
· define and give examples of renewable and nonrenewable resources

What I Learned:
· Coal contains the energy trapped in plants that died millions of years ago.
· Common fossil fuels: coal, oil, gas
· Oil and gas are formed from ocean animals and plants
· Renewable: can be replaced, like lumber; nonrenewable: can't be replaced, like coal

My Six-Hat Thinking Plan

Objective: To motivate students, elicit their background knowledge, focus their attention, and give them practice with summarizing

Grouping: Independent or partners

What to Do: You can use this activity before reading or afterward as a summary. Edward DeBono is the author of *Six Thinking Hats*. Explain to your students that each hat color represents a different kind of thinking.

White hat:	Facts about a topic
Red hat:	Feelings about a topic (emotion)
Yellow hat:	Positive things about a topic
Black hat:	Judging a topic (the disadvantages and problems)
Green hat:	Other thoughts; new ideas, creativity
Blue hat:	Summary of the whole topic

Before reading: List the hat descriptions on the chalkboard and provide each student with a copy of the reproducible on page 20 to fill in before they begin reading. When students are finished, go over these as a class. The discussion and any further questions will help students understand what to look for as they read and remember what they've learned. (See the taxes example.)

Name Bryan

My Six-Hat Thinking Plan

Topic/Title Taxes

White hat
(Facts) Taxes are a percent of money citizens pay to the government. The government collects the taxes and uses the money for roads, schools, armed forces, and so on.

Red hat
(Feelings) I feel taxes are too high and burden the poor.

Yellow hat
(Advantages) Taxes are necessary in order for us to have good roads, schools, etc.

Black hat
(Disadvantages) Sometimes taxes are too high. Some tax money is wasted.

Green hat
(New Ideas) If we eliminated taxes, people would have more control over their money.

Blue hat
(Summary) Taxes are paid by citizens to the government so the government can provide services such as schools, roads, and programs.

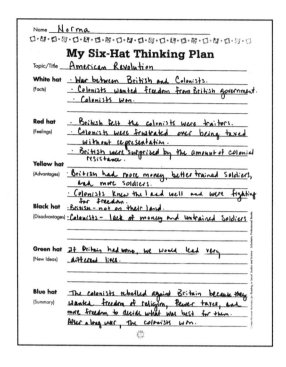

After reading: You can create a more detailed version of the My Six-Hat Thinking Plan after-reading sheet to fit the topic you're studying (See the American Revolution sheet shown here.) After reading about the American Revolution, students write down their thinking for each of the six hats. I used this as an assessment of their learning.

Name __Norma__

My Six-Hat Thinking Plan

Topic/Title __American Revolution__

White hat
(Facts)
· War between British and Colonists.
· Colonists wanted freedom from British government.
· Colonists won.

Red hat
(Feelings)
· British felt the colonists were traitors.
· Colonists were frustrated over being taxed without representation.
· British were surprised by the amount of colonial resistance.

Yellow hat
(Advantages)
· British had more money, better trained soldiers, and more soldiers.
· Colonists knew the land well and were fighting for freedom.

Black hat
(Disadvantages)
· British - not on their land.
· Colonists - lack of money and untrained soldiers

Green hat
(New Ideas)
If Britain had won, we would lead very different lives.

Blue hat
(Summary)
The colonists rebelled against Britain because they wanted freedom of religion, fewer taxes, and more freedom to decide what was best for them. After a long war, the colonists won.

Create-a-Web

Objective: To motivate students and elicit their prior knowledge

Grouping: Independent or small groups

What to Do: This is a variation on the Concept Web activity on page 12. Rather than creating a web for students, create a web together on an overhead or on the chalkboard. Randomly present a list of terms that will be mentioned in the upcoming reading. In groups or individually, have students organize these words into a web according to how they think the words relate to one another. This is a prediction activity, so accept all answers. After the reading, students can correct their web and add terms based on their new knowledge. Ask students to use pencil so they can erase their corrections neatly. Discuss the changes students made.

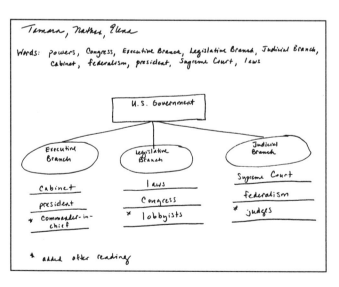

The United States Government web was designed so that students could use their background knowledge to sort a list of vocabulary I gave them. After reading, they corrected their webs with a pen. It was a great learning experience!

Questions and Answers

Objective: To motivate students, elicit their prior knowledge, give them a chance to reflect on what they've learned, and give them practice with summarizing

Grouping: Independent, partners, or small groups

What to Do: Have students preview the reading text. Then, on the Questions and Answers worksheet (page 21), have them write down four (or more) questions they have about the topic or passage. After they read, they should answer their questions in the spaces provided. They wrap up what they've learned from the passage with a summary. Finally, give students time to reflect on the reading passage: How can they apply it to their lives? What lessons did they learn? How is the information related to other facts that they know? Have them write their thoughts in the section called My reaction. Students may have to use other sources to find the answers to their questions.

Partners in Reading

Objective: For students to work together and learn by previewing, reading, and summarizing; to write a response to the reading that relates it to their own lives

Grouping: Partners

What to Do: Provide pairs of students with a copy of the worksheet on page 22. Have partners preview the reading material and write a prediction about what they might learn from it. Then, after looking at the visuals within that reading section, each partner chooses a visual he or she wants to know more about. Next, the partners read the selection. Partner 1 writes a summary of the reading selection while Partner 2 writes one or two questions about the reading selection. Afterward, each partner writes a short reflection on the passage—giving their feelings and opinions about what they've read.

Unit Prep

Objective: To motivate students, elicit their prior knowledge, and build vocabulary

Grouping: Independent or small group

What to Do: I use this strategy before every teaching unit and as follow-up after the unit. After I introduce the unit, the class discusses the topic together, and each student fills out a Unit Prep sheet (page 23), leaving the "What I know I learned" section blank. I provide the information that goes in the "What I will learn" space. I collect the sheets and keep them until we finish the unit. Students can then fill in the "What I know I learned" space.

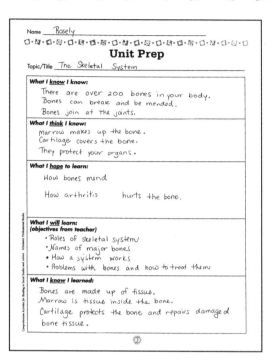

Name Rosely

Unit Prep

Topic/Title The Skeletal System

What I _know_ I know:
There are over 200 bones in your body.
Bones can break and be mended.
Bones join at the joints.

What I _think_ I know:
Marrow makes up the bone.
Cartilage covers the bone.
They protect your organs.

What I _hope_ to learn:
How bones mend
How arthritis hurts the bone.

What I _will_ learn:
(objectives from teacher)
• Roles of skeletal system
• Names of major bones
• How a system works
• Problems with bones and how to treat them

What I _know_ I learned:
Bones are made up of tissue.
Marrow is tissue inside the bone.
Cartilage protects the bone and repairs damaged bone tissue.

VOCABULARY STRATEGIES

Sensible Sentences

Objective: To motivate students, elicit their prior knowledge, and build vocabulary

Grouping: Small groups, then whole class

What to Do: From the text students will be reading, choose six to eight challenging words and four to six words that are more familiar to the students. For example, with a text on earthquakes, you might choose these harder words: *fault, magma, tectonic plate, igneous, metamorphic,* and *sedimentary,* and these easier words: *earthquake, lava, crust, rock,* and *erupt.* List the words on the chalkboard or overhead, and write a definition for each. Give small groups of students copies of the worksheet on page 24. Direct students to think about the topic of the reading and use the words on the list to come up with sentences that might be in the chapter. Each sentence must include at least two of the ten to fourteen words. Put the student contributions on the chalkboard; then have the class read the chapter. Following the reading, go back to each sentence on the board, and discuss with the whole class whether it could or could not be true, based on their reading. If it could not be true, have the class decide how to change it.

Name Jordan

Sensible Sentences

Topic/Title Simple Machines

1 Words: fulcrum, tool
Possible sentence before reading: All tools have fulcrums.

New sentence after reading (if the above is not a true sentence):
Tools that are levers have fulcrums.

2 Words: lever, tool
Possible sentence before reading: Some tools have a lever.

New sentence after reading (if the above is not a true sentence):
A hammer is an example of a tool that is a lever.

3 Words: pulley, machine
Possible sentence before reading: Some machines have pulleys.

New sentence after reading (if the above is not a true sentence):
A pulley is an example of a simple machine.

4 Words: inclined, plane
Possible sentence before reading: The plane landed on the inclined ramp.

New sentence after reading (if the above is not a true sentence):
A screwdriver is a kind of inclined plane.

Cloze It!

Objective: To motivate students, elicit their prior knowledge, and build vocabulary

Grouping: Partners or small groups

What to Do: Students love to guess the word that goes in the blanks. Choose a paragraph from the text they're getting ready to read, and turn it into a fill-in-the-blank challenge by deleting some key vocabulary words. In a Word Bank section, list all of the words that would be used to fill in the blanks. Give each student a copy of the paragraph to complete before they read. After they read the selection, discuss the word choices as a class. Have students cross out the words they filled in incorrectly and write the correct ones above. This will help them remember what the words mean and what they've learned.

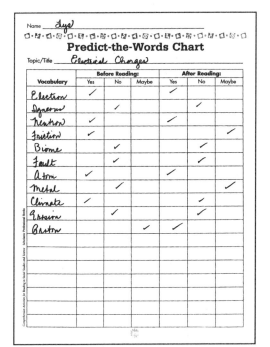

Name _Maria_

Cloze It! for Chapter 7

Use these words to fill in the blanks.

Parliament
Taxes
Boston Tea Party
boycott
French & Indian

After the _French & Indian_ War, King George III taxed the colonists heavily saying that he needed more money because of the cost of this war. The colonists were forced to pay _taxes_ to Britain even though they had no representation in _Parliament_, the governing body in Britain that makes the laws. They refused to pay a tea tax, which caused the _Boston Tea Party_ They especially hated the tax law called the Stamp Act that forced the colonists to _boycott_ stamped goods.

Predict-the-Words Chart

Objective: To motivate students, elicit their prior knowledge, and build vocabulary

Grouping: Whole class or small groups

What to Do: This prediction strategy, which I learned from my friend Mary Howard, encourages children to be discriminating about how words relate to a topic and helps them to become acquainted with difficult vocabulary words before they read. Tell students the topic of your lesson or reading, and then write on the chalkboard several words (some that are within the text of your lesson and some that are not). Have students write the words on their own prediction sheet (page 25) and for each check yes, no, or maybe, according to whether or not they think it will be in that day's lesson. Then tell students to note words on their chart as they encounter them while reading. At the conclusion of the reading, return to the chart to discuss students' predictions.

Name _Lya_

Predict-the-Words Chart

Topic/Title _Electrical Charges_

Vocabulary	Before Reading:			After Reading:		
	Yes	No	Maybe	Yes	No	Maybe
Electron	✓			✓		
Igneous		✓			✓	
Neutron	✓			✓		
Friction	✓					✓
Biome		✓			✓	
Fault		✓			✓	
Atom	✓			✓		
Metal		✓				✓
Climate	✓				✓	
Gaseous		✓			✓	
Boston			✓	✓		

Name _____

Predict-o-Fact

Topic/Title _____

Take a picture and subheading walk through the book or chapter you are about to read, looking for clues to what it is about.

1. On each line below write a prediction sentence.

2. For each prediction put a check mark on the "Before Reading" true or false line according to what you think.

3. Read the selection.

4. Now put a check mark on the "After Reading" true or false line according to what you learned about each prediction.

5. Finally, write a corrected version of each false prediction on the line at the right.

Before Reading	Prediction	After Reading	Corrected Predictions
True False		True False	
— —	_____	— —	_____
— —	_____	— —	_____
— —	_____	— —	_____
— —	_____	— —	_____
— —	_____	— —	_____

What's New?

Topic/Title _____

What I Know:

What I'll Find Out:

What I Learned:

Name _____

My Six-Hat Thinking Plan

Topic/Title _____

White hat　　_____

(Facts)　　　　　_____

　　　　　　　　_____

　　　　　　　　_____

Red hat　　　_____

(Feelings)　　　　_____

　　　　　　　　_____

　　　　　　　　_____

Yellow hat　　_____

(Advantages)　　　_____

　　　　　　　　_____

　　　　　　　　_____

Black hat　　_____

(Disadvantages)　_____

　　　　　　　　_____

　　　　　　　　_____

Green hat　　_____

(New Ideas)　　　_____

　　　　　　　　_____

　　　　　　　　_____

Blue hat　　　_____

(Summary)　　　　_____

　　　　　　　　_____

　　　　　　　　_____

Comprehension Activities for Reading in Social Studies and Science　Scholastic Professional Books

Name _____

Questions and Answers

Topic/Title _____

Before Reading	Question 1
	Question 2
	Question 3
	Question 4

New questions I have after reading:

After Reading	Answer 1
	Answer 2
	Answer 3
	Answer 4

Other information that I learned while reading:

Summary	My reaction:

Comprehension Activities for Reading in Social Studies and Science   Scholastic Professional Books

Partners in Reading

Topic/Title _____

	Partner 1: _____	Partner 2: _____
Prediction		
Most interesting visual in the reading and why		
Summary (1) and Questions (2)		
Reflection		

Comprehension Activities for Reading in Social Studies and Science Scholastic Professional Books

Unit Prep

Topic/Title _____

What I <u>know</u> I know:
What I <u>think</u> I know:
What I <u>hope</u> to learn:
What I <u>will</u> learn: ***(objectives from teacher)***
What I <u>know</u> I learned:

Name _____

Sensible Sentences

Topic/Title _____

1 Words: _____

Possible sentence before reading: _____

_____

New sentence after reading (if the above is not a true sentence):

_____

_____

2 Words: _____

Possible sentence before reading: _____

_____

New sentence after reading (if the above is not a true sentence):

_____

_____

3 Words: _____

Possible sentence before reading: _____

_____

New sentence after reading (if the above is not a true sentence):

_____

_____

4 Words: _____

Possible sentence before reading: _____

_____

New sentence after reading (if the above is not a true sentence):

_____

_____

Comprehension Activities for Reading in Social Studies and Science   Scholastic Professional Books

Name _____

Predict-the-Words Chart

Topic/Title _____

Vocabulary	Before Reading:			After Reading:		
	Yes	No	Maybe	Yes	No	Maybe

Comprehension Activities for Reading in Social Studies and Science   Scholastic Professional Books

Chapter Two

During (and Right After) Reading Strategies

There are several ways to read expository texts: silent reading, teacher read aloud, guided reading, and oral reading by students. You can use the following strategies with all of these approaches to reading. They give students the opportunity to interact with the text and improve reading comprehension.

Mind Mapping

Objective: To help students to organize their thinking while reading and see the relationships among concepts

Grouping: Small groups

What to Do: Have students categorize and organize concepts as they are reading. By seeing how vocabulary and concepts are related, they'll comprehend what they've read. Here are two types of mapping:

1. Picture Labeling

In advance, prepare pictures and graphic organizers relevant to the unit or topic the class will be studying. For example, for a unit on weather, I provide each child with a Weather Vocabulary Packet. It contains a number of pages for the children to label and fill in during a reading session—as they read and immediately afterwards. This technique helps them organize the massive amounts of information they're being exposed to.

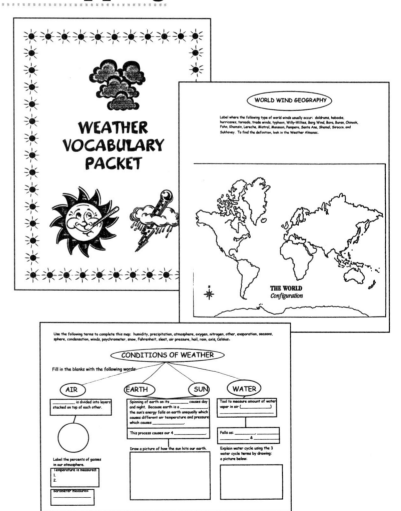

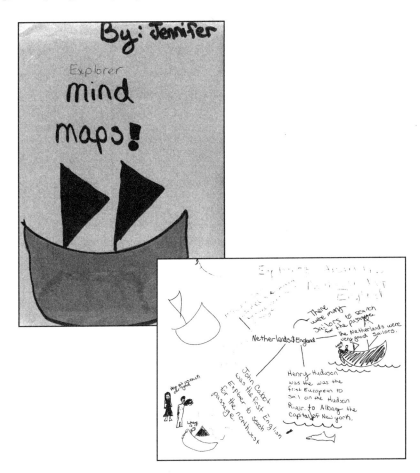

2. Chapter Mapping

As students read a chapter (or maybe even a paragraph, for practice), have them create a map showing the topic and all of the supporting details. Encourage them to be creative. They might use colored pencils to distinguish between categories, draw pictures to represent words, and draw lines between facts or bits of information to show relationships. Explain that there's no need to use complete sentences, but the information must make sense to a reader.

I start off my Explorer Unit by teaching students how to use their social studies textbooks as resources and how to preview them effectively for better comprehension (see Textbook Preview, page 8). Then, as students read, they make a Chapter Map for each section. They're organizing their reading as they go.

Concept Wall

Objective: To review social studies and science vocabulary

Grouping: Whole class

What to Do: Before beginning a unit of study, hang on the classroom wall a large sheet of paper to be used for a web of all the concepts students will learn and how they are related. As students read the various chapters or selections, add to the web. When you've finished the unit, review the web as a class and add and rearrange concepts as needed. I keep the completed Concept-Wall poster up all year long so students can reflect on what they've learned from previous units. For difficult units, I create the web ahead of time so students can see where we're going and how it all connects.

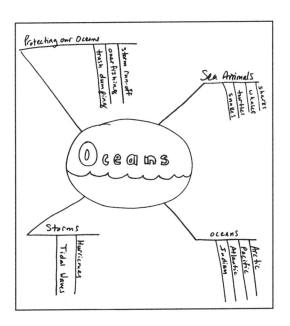

Main Idea Table

Objective: For students to be able to find the main idea of a paragraph

Grouping: Independent or small groups

What to Do: This graphic organizer visually shows children how the main idea (tabletop) always has supporting ideas (legs) to hold it up. Use the Main Idea Table (page 35) to illustrate the difference between the main idea and supporting ideas. Explain that the main idea is usually within the first couple of sentences of a paragraph, and that the supporting sentences, which follow it, provide details. With students, fill in several Main Idea Tables for paragraphs in your expository texts. Provide students with blank copies they can use to analyze specific paragraphs. Discuss these with the whole class or a group of children.

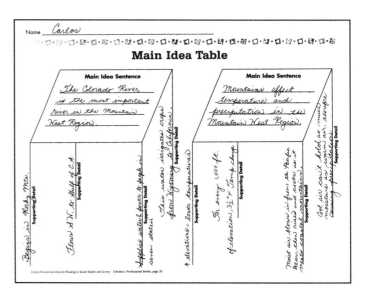

Web It!

Objective: For students to reinforce what they're reading and learning by paraphrasing the reading selection for another student.

Grouping: Partners or small groups

What to Do: Provide copies of Web It! (page 36) to pairs of students. Explain that the topic goes in the large center circle. The main ideas go in the smaller circles and the details go on the radiating lines. Have the partners discuss and web the information while they read. The partners take turns writing a main idea and its details but must agree on what is written.

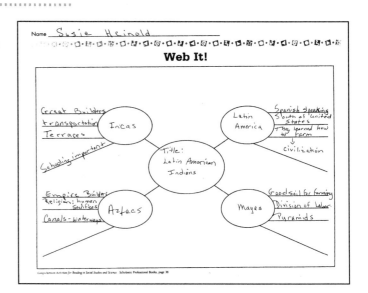

QUADS (Question, Answer, Details)

Objective: For students to reinforce their understanding of what they're reading by developing questions and sharing answers

Grouping: Independent, then groups of four

What to Do: Provide each student with a Quad sheet (page 37). As students read the text individually, they write four questions about the reading, one in each box. Have them write their name above each question and cut the questions apart. Then have students work in groups of four. Each member of the group distributes his or her questions to the other group members (one to two people and two to one person). Every student in the group should end up with four questions to answer. When a student has answered a question (using the book), he or she returns the small sheet to its author. After the authors have all their answered questions back, they read them aloud to the group and discuss whether or not the answers are correct. If an answer is incorrect, the author corrects it. Have students write a detail relevant to the topic after the answer.

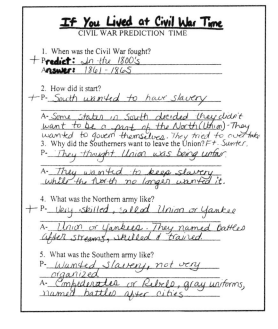

Predict Answer

Objective: To motivate students and draw their attention to particular points

Grouping: Independent

What to Do: Provide each student with a Predict Answer sheet you've created for a reading selection. An example for *If You Lived at the Time of the Civil War* is shown here. While you are reading the book aloud, have students predict an answer for each question and write it in the *P* space. Tell them to guess if they don't know the answer. Read each question and wait until students write their predictions for the answer. Then share one or two predictions with the whole class. Next, read and discuss the answer. Tell students to write down the real answer and put a plus mark next to their prediction if it was correct. Students can't wait to see if their prediction was correct.

You can do this with any reading selection. Just have the questions broken down by paragraph.

INSERT! Code My Thinking

(Interactive Notation System for Effective Reading and Thinking, Vaughn & Estes, 1986)

Objective: For students to reflect, question, and gain new insights by using a coding system as they read

Grouping: Independent, then group or whole-class discussion

What to Do: If it's permissible, photocopy the reading material so that students can respond to it by writing code symbols next to the sentences or paragraphs as they read. Or have students fold a separate piece of paper over the margin beside the material so that they can respond on it. Students can use the code below or develop INSERT symbols of their own. They might enjoy using colored pencils and highlighters.

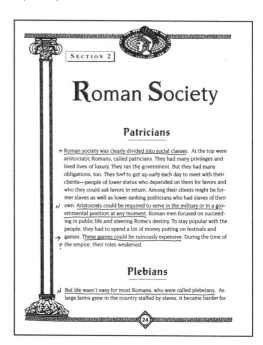

+	I understand	N	New Information
?	I don't understand	*	Very important
<->	Had to reread—difficult at first, but now I understand		
->	I want to share or discuss		

After the students have finished reading and coding, ask them to share one of their insertion marks with the class and talk about their responses. This strategy is a great discussion tool!

Spinner Reading Guide

Objective: For students to focus on the important aspects of the text

Grouping: Groups of two or three

What to Do: Give each group a Reading Spinner (page 38). Start students reading in groups of two or three and have them stop after a subsection or when you yell out "Spin Time." Have one student spin by holding a paper clip in place with a pencil tip on the center point and spinning it loosely with a finger. According to where the paper clip points, the student summarizes the text, formulates a question, clarifies

Pull out
paper clip
as shown:

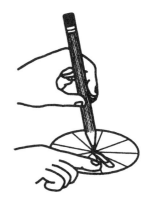

text or a visual, or predicts what will come next. All students should have a turn spinning and responding with the required activity. (If the spinner lands on a section that someone else has already responded to, the student must respond again, using his or her own words.) When everyone has had a turn to spin and speak, have the small groups continue reading until the next stopping point. I usually have students stop and spin after each subheading in the social studies or science book.

Beach ball for Non-fiction

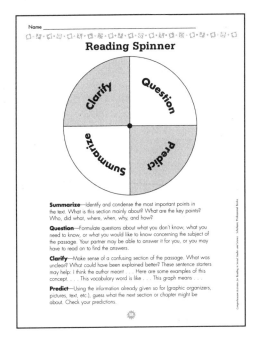

Summarize—Identify and condense the most important points in the text. What is this section mainly about? What are the key points? Who, did what, where, when, why, and how?

Question—Formulate questions about what you don't know, what you need to know, or what you would like to know concerning the subject of the passage. Your partner may be able to answer it for you, or you may have to read on to find the answers.

Clarify—Make sense of a confusing section of the passage. What was unclear? What could have been explained better? These sentence starters may help: I think the author meant . . . Here are some examples of this concept. . . . This vocabulary word is like . . . This graph means . . .

Predict—Using the information already given so far (graphic organizers, pictures, text, etc.), guess what the next section or chapter might be about. Check your predictions.

PULLING IT ALL TOGETHER

Partner Paraphrasing

Objective: For students to summarize what they have read and to learn by hearing another person's understanding of the text

Grouping: Partners

What to Do: Partners read the text about a particular concept (for example rationing, as shown in the example at right) separately. Give each student a sheet of lined paper, folded vertically. Partner 1 writes a summary of the reading on the left side of the paper and folds the written section back so that Partner 2 can't read it. Then, Partner 2 writes his or her summary on the right side of the paper. The two compare their summaries and then write one together. This third cooperative summary cannot be a direct copy of either partner's summary. It must be a combination or rewording of the two summaries.

I Have Learned...

Objective: For students to be able to summarize concisely in writing

Grouping: Independent, then partners

What to Do: As they read, have students fill in the My Creation section of the I Have Learned . . . sheet (page 39). Students write three factual statements after each "that," one question about the content after the word "wonder," and the most important fact or statement after the word "forget." Encourage students to fill these in while they read the text. Next, have students share their I Have Learned . . . sheets with five classmates. Invite students to listen to what the others have learned and take notes, and then go back to write a Shared Creation, including additional information and thoughts from the five other students' I Have Learned. . . sheets. Then have students create a final version with the new information they received from the other five students. Have students either type this final copy or write it very neatly on colored paper. Encourage the students to create an artistic border around the text. Then, bind all of these sheets to form a class book. Students love finding their information in other's final copies.

Ask Yourself...

Objective: For students to be able to summarize a reading selection by asking themselves the journalism questions: Who? Did what? Where? When? Why? And how?

Grouping: Independent

What to Do: Have students use the Ask Yourself . . . strategy to summarize what they read by asking themselves these six questions. Who? Did What? Where? When? Why? And how? As they answer the questions, students are organizing the information. This is also a great way to summarize historical events in a social studies book.

How Am I Doing?

Objective: To assess why students are not comprehending expository text by learning which strategies they are using and which they are not using

Grouping: Partners

What to Do: Give each student a Strategy Choice sheet (page 40). While Partner 1 is reading aloud, Partner 2 documents which strategy the reader is using by placing tally marks in the appropriate Partner 1 slots. After Partner 1 has read a section or several paragraphs, Partner 2 starts reading, and Partner 1 documents which strategies Partner 2 is using. When both students have read and documented the whole passage, each partner should fill in his or her Self Reflection section. Collect the sheets and make two photocopies so that you have the original, and both partners can have a copy. Over time, collect several of these completed sheets from each student so that when reading problems arise you can see which strategies any particular student needs to work on and which are strengths. You may also wish to use these sheets at parent conferences.

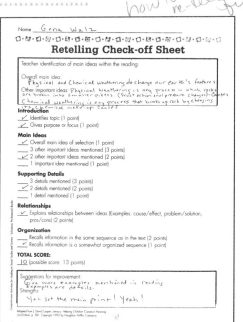

Retelling Check-off Sheet

Objective: To assess the student's reading comprehension

Grouping: Independent, with the teacher

What to Do: First, on a copy of the Retelling Check-off Sheet (page 41) write down the overall main idea and other important ideas in the reading selection. Refer to these as you meet with students individually. After a student reads the selection (either silently or aloud), ask, "Can you retell what you just read to me? Include as many details as possible." Put a check mark next to the appropriate statements. For example, if he or she mentions two main ideas put a check in that space. If he or she mentions the relationship between two ideas, check that space, and so on. Add the points up. Then share the results with the student. Talk about the passage, the student's insights, and the score. Have students set goals to improve their scores.

What's Important?

Objective: To analyze and test students' concept attainment and word categorization

Grouping: Whole class, then independent or small groups

What to Do: This strategy is based on the Frayer model. On the center of a transparency made from the What's Important? sheet (page 42), write a key word from the text and a contextual sentence using it. Ask the class to tell you the essential characteristics of the thing or concept—what other words describe it. Then, ask for some non-essential characteristics. Finally, ask the students to brainstorm examples and non-examples of the key word. Write down all these student-suggested contributions as students say them. After your students have helped fill out the class model, they'll be ready to complete their own sheet. Assign each student the same word or different words to use.

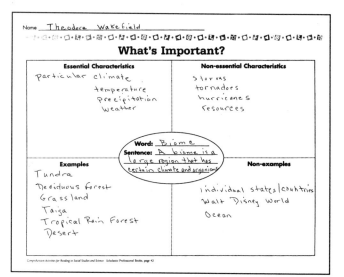

You can have students fill out the sheet before reading to stimulate their background knowledge and then add to it after reading to reinforce what they've learned. Or you can use the sheet just after the reading as a review of the key word and its meaning.

Main Idea Table

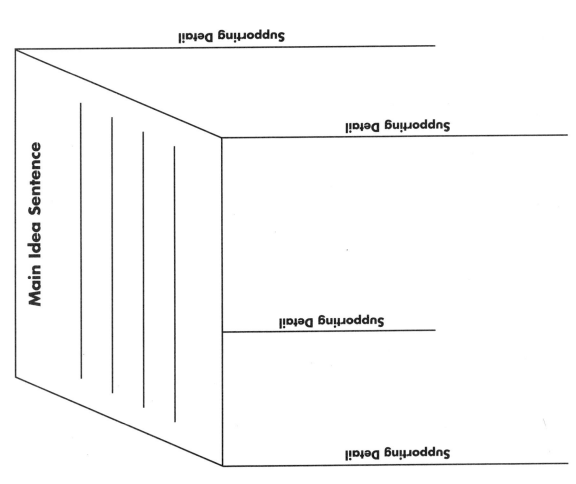

Main Idea Sentence

Supporting Detail

Supporting Detail

Supporting Detail

Supporting Detail

Main Idea Sentence

Supporting Detail

Supporting Detail

Supporting Detail

Supporting Detail

Name _____

Web It!

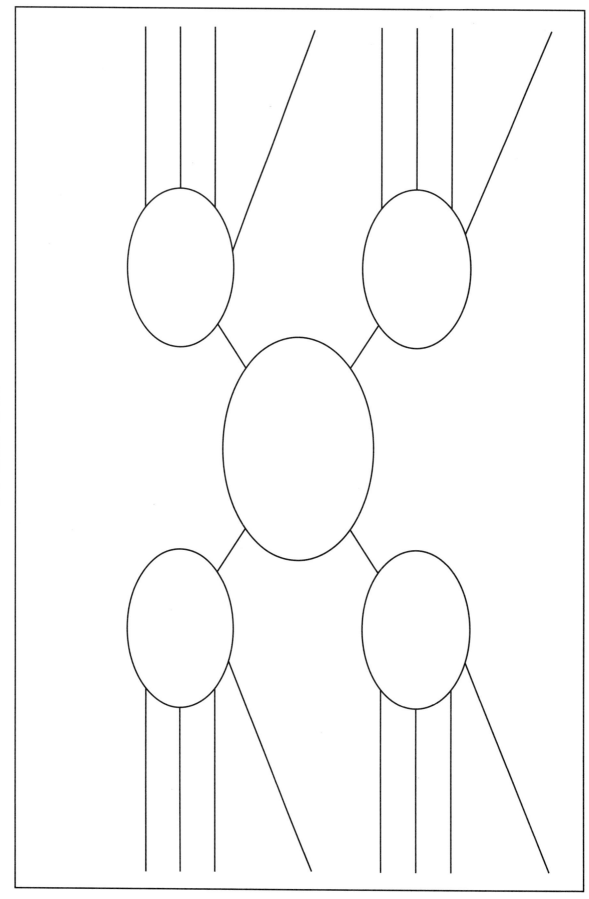

QUADS

Author: _____

Question:

Answer:

Author: _____

Question:

Answer:

Author: _____

Question:

Answer:

Author: _____

Question:

Answer:

Reading Spinner

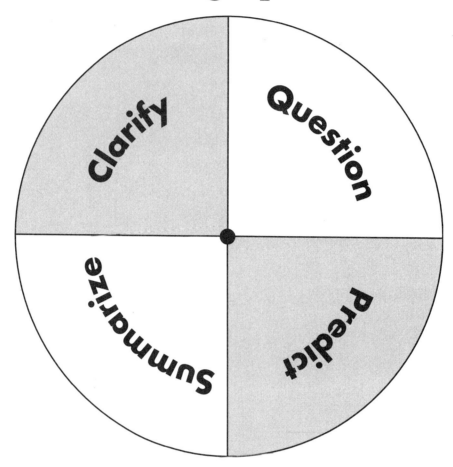

Summarize—Identify and condense the most important points in the text. What is this section mainly about? What are the key points? Who, did what, where, when, why, and how?

Question—Formulate questions about what you don't know, what you need to know, or what you would like to know concerning the subject of the passage. Your partner may be able to answer it for you, or you may have to read on to find the answers.

Clarify—Make sense of a confusing section of the passage. What was unclear? What could have been explained better? These sentence starters may help: I think the author meant . . . Here are some examples of this concept. . . . This vocabulary word is like . . . This graph means . . .

Predict—Using the information already given so far (graphic organizers, pictures, text, etc.), guess what the next section or chapter might be about. Check your predictions.

Comprehension Activities for Reading in Social Studies and Science Scholastic Professional Books

Name _____

I Have Learned ...

Topic: _____

MY CREATION:

I have learned that: _____

_____

that: _____

_____

that: _____

_____

Now, I wonder: _____

_____

I will never forget: _____

_____

SHARED CREATION FROM: (list 5 names)

I have learned from _____ that: _____

_____

from _____ that: _____

_____

from _____ that: _____

_____

from _____ that: _____

_____

Now, I wonder: _____

_____

and _____

I will never forget: _____

_____

and _____

Comprehension Activities for Reading in Social Studies and Science   Scholastic Professional Books

Name _____

Strategy Choice

Strategy	Partner 1	Partner 2
1. Predicted		
2. Thought about a word		
3. Reread		
4. Summarized		
5. Asked a question		
6. Connected to prior knowledge		
7. Other: _____		

Self Reflection

Partner 1:

Today, I feel that my comprehension was (poor, okay, excellent) because:

_____

_____

Things I can do tomorrow in order to comprehend better:

1.

2.

3.

Partner 2:

Today, I feel that my comprehension was (poor, okay, excellent) because:

_____

_____

Things I can do tomorrow in order to comprehend better:

1.

2.

3.

Comprehension Activities for Reading in Social Studies and Science   Scholastic Professional Books

Name _____

Retelling Check-off Sheet

Teacher identification of main ideas within the reading:

Overall main idea:

Other important ideas:

Introduction
____ Identifies topic (1 point)
____ Gives purpose or focus (1 point)

Main Ideas
____ Overall main idea of selection (1 point)
____ 3 other important ideas mentioned (3 points)
____ 2 other important ideas mentioned (2 points)
____ 1 important idea mentioned (1 point)

Supporting Details
____ 3 details mentioned (3 points)
____ 2 details mentioned (2 points)
____ 1 detail mentioned (1 point)

Relationships
____ Explains relationships between ideas (Examples: cause/effect, problem/solution, pros/cons) (2 points)

Organization
____ Recalls information in the same sequence as in the text (2 points)
____ Recalls information is a somewhat organized sequence (1 point)

TOTAL SCORE:
____ (possible score: 13 points)

Suggestions for improvement:

Strengths:

Adapted from J. David Cooper, *Literacy: Helping Children Construct Meaning.*
2nd Edition, p. 581. Copyright 1993 by Houghton Mifflin Company.

What's Important?

Non-essential Characteristics

Essential Characteristics

Word: _____
Sentence: _____

Examples

Non-examples

Chapter Three

After-Reading Projects and Activities

Now that your students have comprehended informational reading materials by jogging their background knowledge, making connections, mentally organizing the material, creating meaning by relating the text to their lives, and summarizing, it's time to revisit and reinforce the material so that they'll be able to commit it to long-term memory. This is where the after-reading activities and projects come in.

Francis Bacon said, "Some books are to be tasted, others are to be swallowed, and some few are to be chewed and digested." Not every reading experience will need a post-reading follow up, but activities or projects that encourage students to do something creative with the information they've just read can enhance and enrich the learning and make it a part of their knowledge and lives.

Michael and Bonnie Graves, in *Scaffolding Reading Experiences*, summed up this process with the following visual:

READ → THINK and ELABORATE ← → RESPOND

Sometimes we read, think and elaborate, and then respond. The response may bring about more thinking and elaborating and thus create deeper understanding. Response to reading can take many forms—speaking, writing, dramatics, art, music, or dance. For post-reading activities, students recall what they've read and demonstrate understanding by applying, synthesizing, evaluating, elaborating, and sharing ideas. "Post-reading activities also provide opportunities for students to extend ideas, to explore new ways of thinking, doing, and seeing—to invent and create, to ponder the question, 'What if?'" (Graves, 115).

The following after-reading activities fall into one or more of these response categories—questioning, discussing, writing, drama or other artistic expression, application activities, and reteaching.

Fact-or-Fiction Flip-ups

Objective: For students to creatively review their reading by writing sentences

Grouping: Partners

What to Do: Have students come up with nine fact or fiction (true or false) statements about what they've read and write them on cut-out square sheets. (Sticky notes work well.) Have students stick the top portion of the squares on a piece of paper so that squares are side by side and can flip up. Then have students exchange the flip-up paper with a partner. The partner then decides whether the statements are true or false by finding the information in the reading source. He or she then flips each square up and writes whether it's true or false beneath it. If it is false, the partner rewrites the statement to make it true. Students may enjoy illustrating some of the statements.

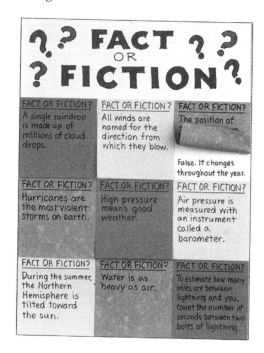

Important Book

Objective: For students to write, analyze, and summarize what's most important about a reading

Grouping: Independent or small groups

What to Do: In *The Important Book* (Harper, 1949), Margaret Wise Brown describes something—a shoe, snow, an apple, and so on—by explaining what is most important about it. For example, she writes: "The important things about a shoe are that you put your foot in it. You walk in it, and you take it off at night . . ." After sharing the book with the class, tell your students to pick the most important thing about the topic they're studying in their textbook or other expository text. Once they've decided, have them

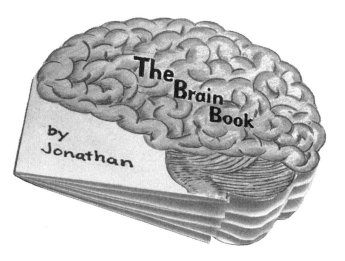

brainstorm a list of details about that point and combine these details into a paragraph. Echoing *The Important Book*, they should repeat the most important thing in the first and last sentences. Share these with the whole class, and put them together in a class book. Students can make their own Most Important Books by combining paragraphs—one to a page—about important points within a section or chapter and illustrating each page.

Fortunately & Unfortunately

Objective: To have students deepen their understanding by analyzing pros and cons

Grouping: Partners or small groups

What to Do: After students read the expository text, read aloud *Fortunately* by Remy Charlip (Simon & Schuster, 1984). Help students notice that this book follows a pattern: "Fortunately one day, Ned got a letter that said, Please come to a surprise party, [*next page*] but unfortunately the party was in Florida and he was in New York." Have students follow this pattern to write "Fortunately and Unfortunately" sentences about the subject of the expository text. Then have partners or small groups create a short story imitating the book pattern, using at least three or four— I recommend a minimum of eight—facts from the expository text. Bind the statements—one to a page—into a book and have the students illustrate the pages.

Fortunately, the government gave U.S. citizens 160 free acres if they settled and farmed the western land for 5 years.

Unfortunately, the hardships on this "hard-to-plant" land were so tough that not many people took advantage of this free offer.

Filmstrip Stories

Objective: To have students reinforce their knowledge by summarizing a series of events in the correct order

Grouping: Independent or partners

What to Do: Distribute several sheets of filmstrip paper (page 51) to each student. Have students use the filmstrip to tell a historical story in the correct chronological order. They write the first fact in the first frame, and so on, and then illustrate each fact. Prepare a viewer (a box with a rectangular window cut out and holes for pencils or dowels to roll the strips on) so the students can show their filmstrips to the whole class. To prepare, have students:

1. Cut out and tape the strips together in the correct order.
2. Tape the ends of the strip to two pencils (or dowels).
3. Roll the strip on the bottom pencil.
4. Position the strip in the viewer with the first frame showing.

You may wish to have each student create a filmstrip for a different event from the twentieth century and share with the class.

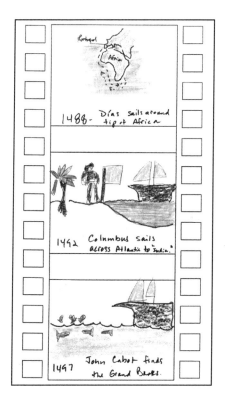

1488- Días sails around tip of Africa

1492 Columbus sails across Atlantic to "India."

1497 John Cabot finds the Grand Banks.

Famous-Figure Photo Album & Scrapbook

Objective: For students to review and augment what they've learned by summarizing and creatively illustrating facts from expository text

Grouping: Independent or partners

What to Do: When you're studying a time period in history, have each student choose a famous or representative figure of that time (great for autobiographies, biographies, or historical fiction) and create a photo album or scrapbook that might have belonged to him or her. To prepare a 10- to 12-page album, have students staple together in book form five or six pieces of long construction paper. Then invite students to take pictures from magazines, newspapers, or the computer or draw their own illustrations to create their person's album.

The character for the sample album shown here was chosen from the book *Number the Stars* by Lois Lowry (Dell Yearling Book, 1990) a piece of historical fiction that contains many facts about the Holocaust.

This is Annemarie at her house on her blue couch. We had to live with her for quite a while. She's wearing my necklace.

Point-of-View Timeline

Objective: For students to think and learn more by sequencing and evaluating what happened during a particular time in history

Grouping: Independent or partners

What to Do: Have students create a timeline that not only shows what happened during a particular time in history, but how it was seen by one of the characters from the time period. For example, students can create a timeline for the American Revolution from a colonist's point of view. (See the example at right.)

If one thing that happened was very positive for the colonists, the event is placed along the +5 line; if somewhat positive around the +4 or +3 line; and so on. I had half of the students create the timeline from the colonists' point of view and the other half from the British point of view.

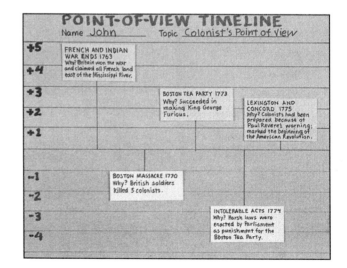

Pop-Up Book Summaries

Objective: For students to creatively display a summary of information they've learned about a particular topic

Grouping: Independent

What to Do: Before I begin a unit for which I'll want students to read several kinds of expository texts, I explain that they should take good notes so that later they'll be able to create a pop-up book that displays what's most important about the topic. Before they start reading, predict with students what facts and ideas will be the most important. For example, before studying the Civil War and reading the historical novel, *Who Comes With Cannons?* by Patricia Beatty (Greenwillow, 1992), we listed some of the things we thought we'd need to look for. After they read, the students used their notes to display their data in pop-up book format. They included a table of contents and some of the following techniques. These could be used for any unit.

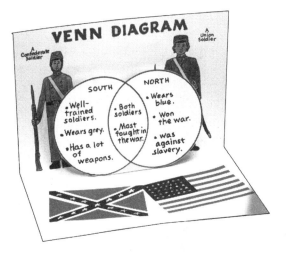

Timeline
Venn diagram comparison
Story web
Best/worst parts
Famous quotes

Advantages/disadvantages
Cause/effect
Character web
Acrostic poetry

Pros/cons
Summary
Vocabulary (illustrated and defined)
Short biographies

Acrostic Poetry

Objective: For students to display the vocabulary they've learned from reading in a creative, meaningful way

Grouping: Small groups

What to Do: Choose one or more main topic words, and for each letter in the word or words have students create a new word related to the topic. The new word can use the letter from anywhere in the main topic word.

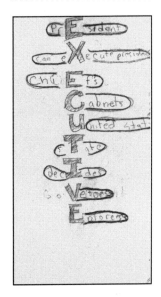

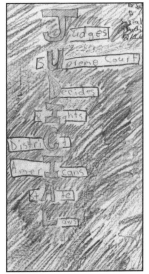

Synectics Similes

Objective: To encourage students to use fluid and creative thinking by comparing things that wouldn't ordinarily be compared

Grouping: Whole class and small groups

What to Do: Synectics, a term coined by industrial psychologists, William Gordon and George Prince, was created for problem solving. *Syn* means "bringing together" and *ectics* means "diverse elements." You can use this strategy as a prewriting activity as well as a review of a newly taught topic. Use the Synectics Similes sheet (page 52) to help students create similes for two objects that are distinct.

1. As a whole class, write the concept or topic you're studying on the Topic line. Then, have students work in small groups of three or four.

2. Ask the groups to brainstorm (and record in the boxes) four words in a particular category that is different from the topic listed above. The category can be anything— things found in a kitchen, ocean words, sports words, foods, and so on. It doesn't matter what category students choose since they're comparing the newly taught topic to a category of familiar words that have no relationship to it.

3. As a whole class, share some of the words that the groups brainstormed. Make sure students understand what a simile is, and try coming up with a few together so they understand the principle. Students can work together or separately on their similes. I recommend working together because this is not an easy task.

4. Tell students they will have one minute to call out as many similes as possibles for the topic word and any of the four categories. When you say "go," the groups (one student writes while the others brainstorm) begin. Say "stop" after three minute. Students may choose to create five similes using one of the words, one using another, three using another, and two using the last word. I just ask that they use all words at least once.

Name __Andrew__

Synectics Similes

Topic __Tornadoes__

Category of Comparison: _____

Octopus	ocean currents
eel	shark

1. A tornado _____ is like a(n) __ocean current__ because they twirl around mixing hot + cold together.

2. A tornado _____ is like a(n) __ocean current__ because they hop around and are unpredictable.

3. A tornado _____ is like a(n) __eel__ because it can have an electric charge to it.

4. A tornado _____ is like a(n) __shark__ because you never know when or where it can attack.

5. A tornado _____ is like a(n) __shark__ because it sneaks up on its prey and kills.

6. A tornado _____ is like a(n) __octopus__ because it grabs objects and gobbles them up.

7. _____ is like a(n) _____ because

3-2-1 Writing Review

Objective: To have students review by summarizing a newly taught topic

Grouping: Independent

What to Do: Have students write down three interesting facts, two questions they still have, and one short opinion paragraph on a sheet of paper. The great thing about this activity is that you can create your own categories of summarization with the numbers 3-2-1. For example, you could ask for three types of rock in the earth's crust and explanations of each, two statistics questions about the earth, and one opinion paragraph about soil conservation. Tailor this summarization activity to the needs of your class and focus it on the topic at hand.

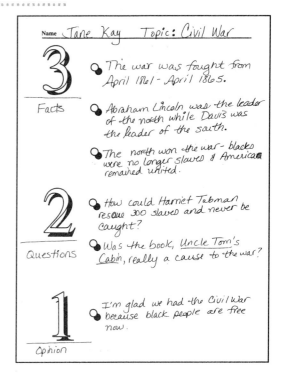

Points of Views (RAFT)

Objective: For students to express what they've learned creatively through a variety of perspectives

Grouping: Individual or whole class

What to Do: The RAFT strategy is based on the work of Rachel Billmeyer and Mary Lee Barton. Begin by telling students that they are going to write summaries about a topic they've just studied, using a strategy called RAFT. The RAFT (Role, Audience, Format, Topic) strategy allows students to process information rather than just writing out answers to questions. Identify the topic (earth, heart, complete sentences, ocean, or whatever you choose).

Explain that:

R stands for **Role**—What is the writer's role (reporter, observer, eyewitness?)

A stands for **Audience**—Who will be reading this writing? (teacher, parent, community)

F stands for **Format**—What is the best way to present this writing? (letter, diary, poem, article)

T stands for **Topic**—Who or what is the subject of this writing? (famous author, heart, inventions, current events)

Next, brainstorm as a whole class 1) roles students might assume for their writing (for the heart topics, students could be a white blood cell or a heart valve and explain their role in making the heart pump, 2) who their audience will be (a heart valve could be writing to the veins or to doctors), and, 3) what the writing format will be (a heart valve could use the complaint form because the doctors didn't know what was wrong with it). Show students a variety of examples so they'll be inspired and won't be limited in coming up with their own ideas.

Point of View (RAFT) Examples

ROLE	AUDIENCE	FORMAT	TOPIC
Lungs	Cigarettes	Complaint	Effects of smoking
George Washington	His wife and family	Letter	American Revolution
Harriet Tubman	Herself	Diary	Underground railroad
Plant	Sun	Thank you note	Sun's role in plant growth
Democratic or Republican lawyer	Supreme Court	Three main ideas and supporting details	2004 election
Vitamin C	Your body	Explanation	How vitamin C is absorbed by the body

Now have each student fill in a small RAFT sheet like the one shown here. I ask that students staple this to their rough draft so that I know their choices.

```
R — Role _____

A — Audience _____

F — Format _____

T — Topic _____
```

Sometimes I choose the format, depending on what we have learned and studied thus far. There are also times when the whole class uses the same RAFT model to write; but most of the time, I allow my students to decide on their own RAFT designations.

Name _____

Filmstrip Pattern

Synectics Similies

Topic _____

Category of Comparison: _____

1 _____ is like a(n) _____ because

_____

2 _____ is like a(n) _____ because

_____

3 _____ is like a(n) _____ because

_____

4 _____ is like a(n) _____ because

_____

5 _____ is like a(n) _____ because

_____

6 _____ is like a(n) _____ because

_____

7 _____ is like a(n) _____ because

_____

Chapter Four

Graphic Organizers for Content Area Texts

Texts are organized in a number of ways, but there are six patterns that appear most often. Research shows that students remember information better if they organize it themselves. By using the graphic organizers described below, students will absorb information as they read, and write it in an organized fashion. Reproducibles for each type of organizer follow.

1. Chronological—organizes events in a time sequence
* Chronological Sequence (page 55)
* Dates on Track (page 56)

2. Compare and Contrast—organizes information about two or more topics according to their similarities and differences.
* Venn Diagram (page 57)
* Similarities and Differences (page 58)

3. Concept Definition and Description—organizes information about a word or phrase that represents a generalized idea of a group of people, places, things, or events. It can also extend the generalized idea by displaying the details that describe the characteristics of the specific people, places, things, or events.
* What's the Big Idea? (page 59)

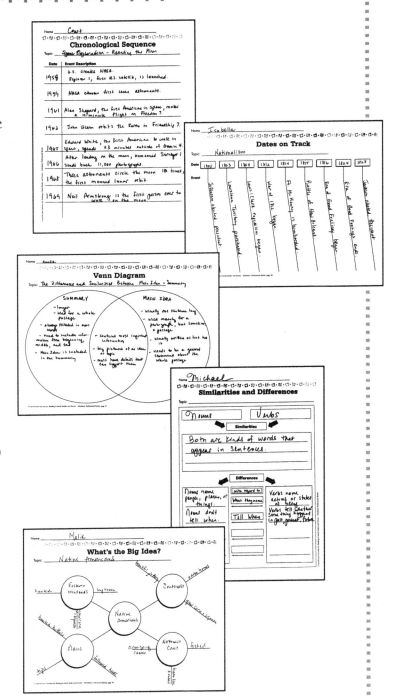

4. Episodic—organizes a large body of information around a specific event. For example: an account of Watergate—when it occurred, who was involved, how long it lasted, the sequence of events, what caused it, and the effects.

✳ Event Explanation (page 60)

5. Cause and Effect—organizes information into a causal sequence that leads to a specific outcome.

✳ Chain of Events (page 61)

✳ The Reasons . . . (page 62)

✳ Single Cause and Effect (page 63)

6. Problem/Solution—organizes information into solutions for a problem or several problems.

✳ Fixing the Problem (page 64)

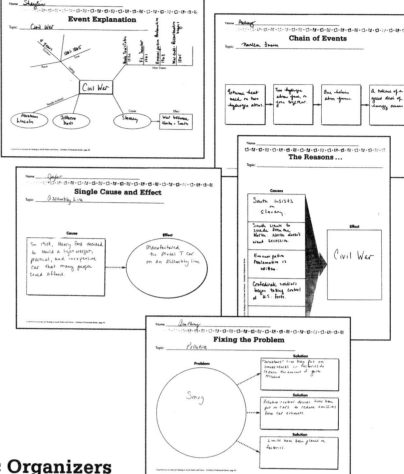

How to Use the Graphic Organizers

Though most expository texts are organized in one of the six ways described, some texts combine two or three of the organizational patterns. You'll need to read the text ahead of time to determine the best graphic organizer or organizers (you may need to use two or three for one reading selection) to give your students. You can usually tell which pattern to use by determining which one would help you organize the information so that you could teach it successfully. Sometimes questions in the teacher's guide will point you in the right direction.

There's no one way to use the graphic organizers. Below are some ideas to choose from. Base your decision on your topic, the time you have, and your goals.

1. Use during reading to organize information.

2. Use before reading to build background knowledge and prepare students for new material.

3. Use after reading to connect the text information with students' prior knowledge.

4. Use as a whole class, independently, in small groups, or with partners.

5. Use as assessments. For example, you provide the wording and students place it correctly within the graphic organizer. Or leave out a part, section, or word, and have the students figure out what belongs in the blank.

Name _____

Chronological Sequence

Topic: _____

Date	Event Description

Comprehension Activities for Reading in Social Studies and Science   Scholastic Professional Books

Name

Dates on Track

Topic:

Date

Event

Name _____

Venn Diagram

Topic: _____

Name _____

Similarities and Differences

Topic: _____

Similarities

Differences

Comprehension Activities for Reading in Social Studies and Science Scholastic Professional Books

What's the Big Idea?

Topic: _____

Name _____

Event Explanation

Topic: _____

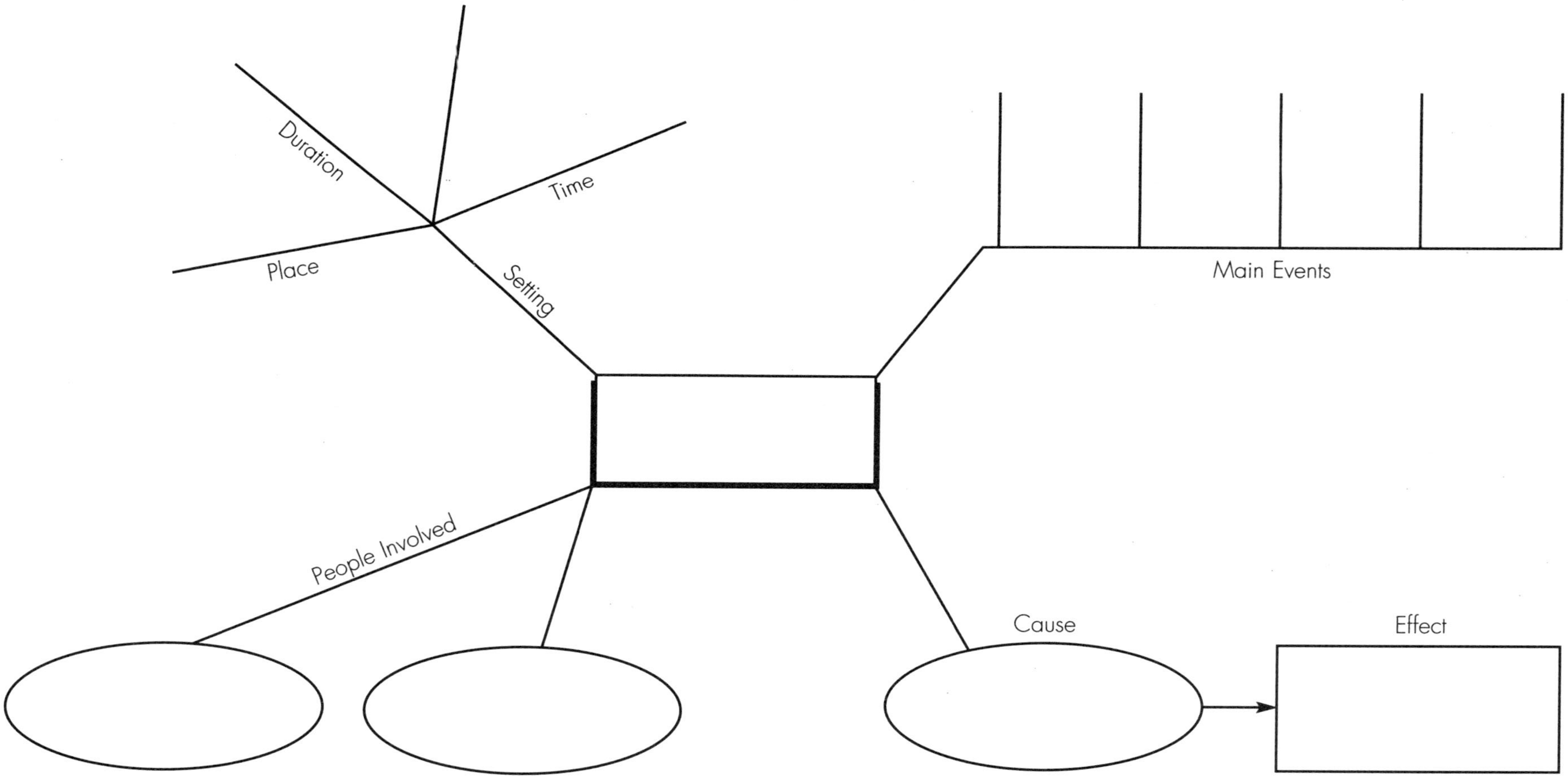

Main Events

Effect

Cause

Time

Setting

Duration

Place

People Involved

Name _____

Chain of Events

Topic: _____

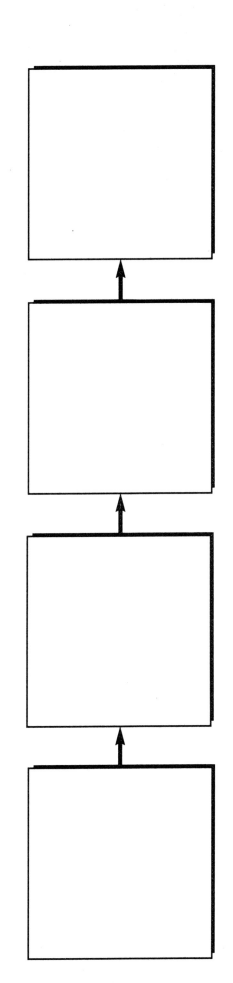

Name _____

The Reasons ...

Topic: _____

Causes

Effect

Name _____

Single Cause and Effect

Topic: _____

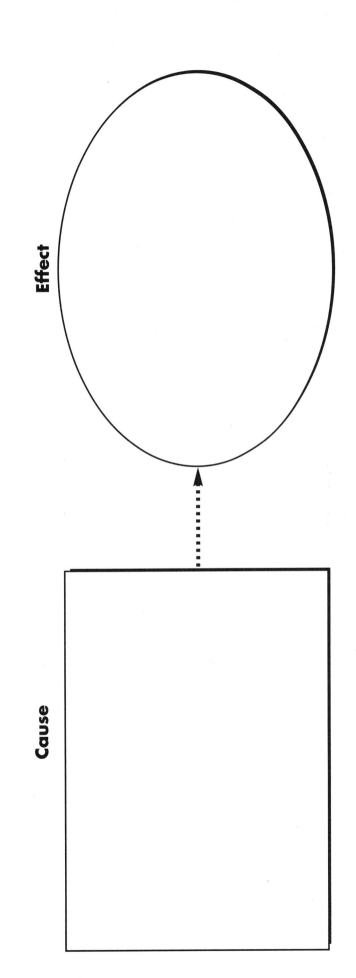

Effect

Cause

Name _____

Fixing the Problem

Topic: _____

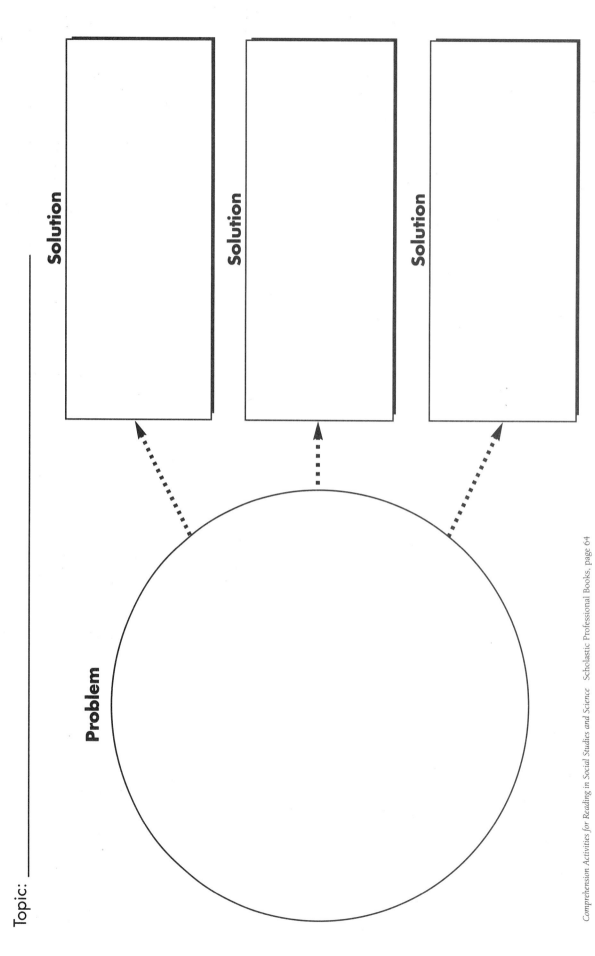

Problem

Solution

Solution

Solution